These Are My Senses

What Can I Feel?

Joanna Issa

Heinemann
LIBRARY

Chicago, Illinois

© 2015 Heinemann Library
an imprint of Capstone Global Library, LLC
Chicago, Illinois

Edited by Siân Smith
Designed by Richard Parker and Peggie Carley
Picture research by Tracy Cummins
Production by Victoria Fitzgerald
Originated by Capstone Global Library Ltd

Library of Congress Cataloging-in-Publication Data
Cataloging-in-publication information is on file with the
Library of Congress.
ISBN 978-1-4846-0432-8 (paperback)
ISBN 978-1-4846-0445-8 (eBook PDF)

Image Credits
Getty Images: JuanSilva, 17, LWA/Dann Tardif, cover,
moxiegirl12, 11, back cover, Salima Senyavskaya, 14, will_
snyder, 7; Shutterstock: auremar, 19, Dhoxax, 12, Diana
Taliun, 16, 20 (left), George Lamson, 4, Igor Kovalchuk,
15, 21 (left), ipag, 6, JCREATION, 8, Monika Gniot, 13,
oksix, 18, 21 (right), Sunny Forest, 10, vidguten, 5, 22 (left),
Whitear, 9, 20 (right), 22 (right)

Contents

What Can I Feel?

Here is a puppy.

It feels **soft**.

Here is some gum.

It feels sticky.

Here is a cactus.

It feels **spiky**.

Here is a tree.

It feels rough.

Here is a flower.

It feels smooth.

Here is a leaf.

It feels rough.

Here is play dough.

It feels soft.

Here is honey.

It feels sticky.

Quiz: Opposite Pairs

Which of these objects feels spiky?

Which of these objects feels sticky?

Picture Glossary

 **soft**

 **spiky**

Index

Notes For Teachers and Parents

BEFORE READING

Build Background:
Have children think of things that are soft to touch and things that are rough.
Which do they like to feel best?

AFTER READING

Recall and reflection:
What things are soft to touch? (puppy, play dough) What things are sticky? (honey, gum)
Would children like to touch something sticky? Why or why not?

Sentence knowledge:
Ask children to look at page 12. How many sentences are on this page?
How can they tell?

Word knowledge (phonics):
Encourage children to point at the word *feels* on page 13. Sound out the four phonemes
in the word *f/ee/l/s*. Ask children to sound out each phoneme as they point at the letters
and then blend the sounds together to make the word *feels*. Challenge them to say some
words that rhyme with *feels*. (heels, meals, peels, wheels)

Word recognition:
Have children point to the word *rough* on page 11. Can they also find it on page 15?

EXTENDING IDEAS
Put a number of small objects in a bag. (toy car, block, soft toy, pencil, eraser, sock) Ask
children to put their hands inside the bag and feel for an object. Can they describe how
it feels to the other children? Can the other children guess what the object is? Let children
pull the object out of the bag to show the class if they were right or wrong.

In This Book

Topic

touch and senses

High-frequency words

a

here

is

it

Sentence stems

1. It feels _____.

2. Here is a _____.